TASTE OF
AFRICA

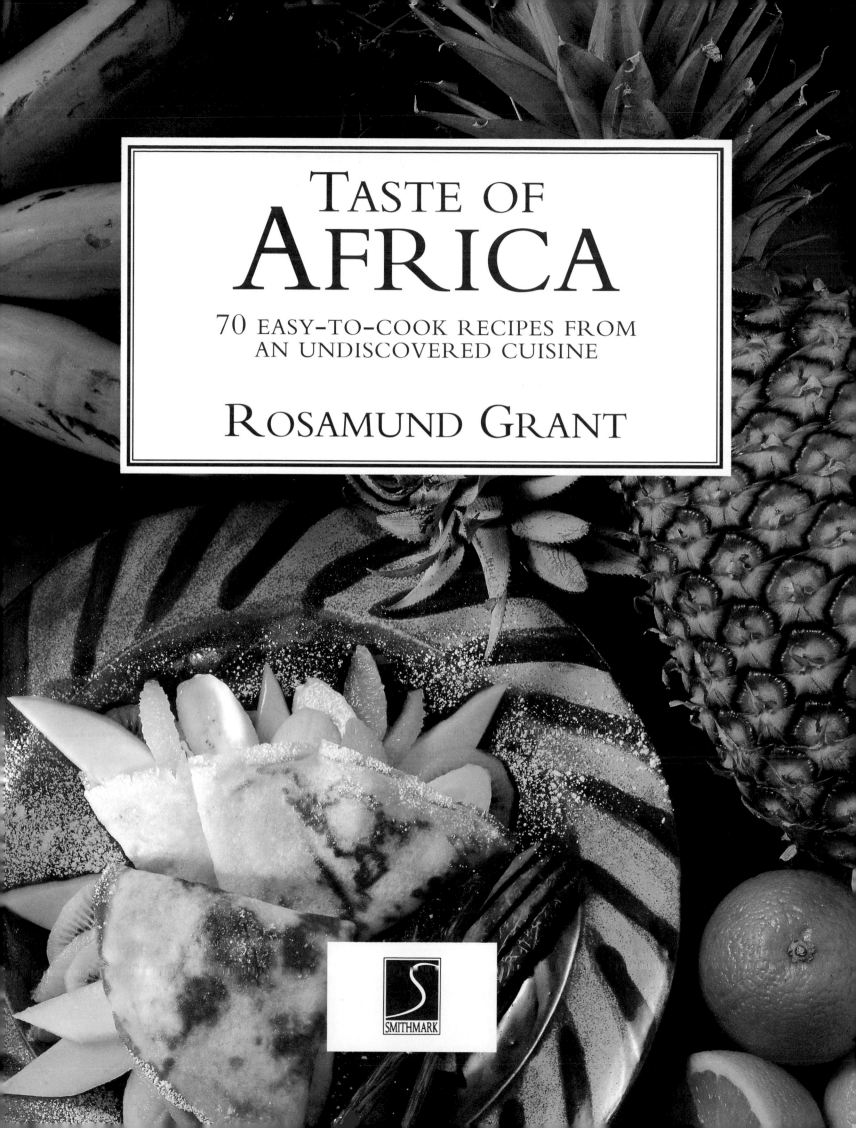

Taste of
AFRICA

70 EASY-TO-COOK RECIPES FROM
AN UNDISCOVERED CUISINE

ROSAMUND GRANT

SMITHMARK

To Patricia Elonge, Nii Noi, Efua, Princess Ajibe Ebanja
and Hazel Ayesha Daniels

This edition published in 1995
by Smithmark Publishers, a division of U.S. Media Holdings, Inc.,
16 East 32nd Street, New York, NY 10016

SMITHMARK books are available for bulk purchase for sales
promotion and premium use. For details write or call the manager of
special sales,
SMITHMARK Publishers,
16 East 32nd Street, New York, NY 10016; (212) 532–6600

ISBN 0-8317-7893-8

Publisher: Joanna Lorenz
Senior Cookery Editor: Linda Fraser
Cookery Editor: Anne Hildyard
Copy Editor: Christine Ingram
Designer: Siân Keogh
Photography and styling: Patrick McLeavey, assisted by Jo Brewer
Food for Photography: Annie Nichols assisted by Curtis Edwards
Illustrator: Madeleine David

Printed in Singapore by Star Standard Industries Pte. Ltd.

10 9 8 7 6 5 4 3 2 1

The author would like to thank all those people who kindly gave their time –
and their recipes: Bethlehem, Ethiopian restaurateur and owner of Senke in
North London, who taught her many traditional dishes from their menu.
Neema Nsubuga, from Bukoba on Lake Victoria in Tanzania,
who helped her with ingredients. Her cousin, Nene Elonge, a talented and
versatile cook, who made exquisite Cameroonian dishes and gave lots
of creative ideas with plantains. She would like to thank Millicent for her
Kenyan recipes, Donu for her lovely Lobster Piri Piri and
advice on Nigerian cooking.
Lastly, Doris and Curtis for helping to test the recipes – and for painstakingly
counting every ounce to achieve accuracy.

Pictures on page 1 and page 7 Zefa Pictures Ltd

CONTENTS

INTRODUCTION

Entertaining with food and music is integral to African social life and family, friends and festivity are closely associated in both rural and urban homes. "No advance warning required" is an attitude that prevails and, in fact, cooking only for the members of your household can get you a bad reputation! So, many hosts and hostesses make it their business to ensure that there are always extra tidbits around for unexpected visitors who might call by at any time of the day or evening.

Foreigners are often amazed by the warmth that is lavished upon them when they only expected a cup of tea!

Rigid recipes are rare, most African cooks inherit vague techniques by word of mouth and then go on to develop their skills by experimenting with different ingredients and cooking methods. They often create new and interesting combinations by following their instincts rather than written instructions. So it isn't too fanciful to talk about cooking that comes from the heart.

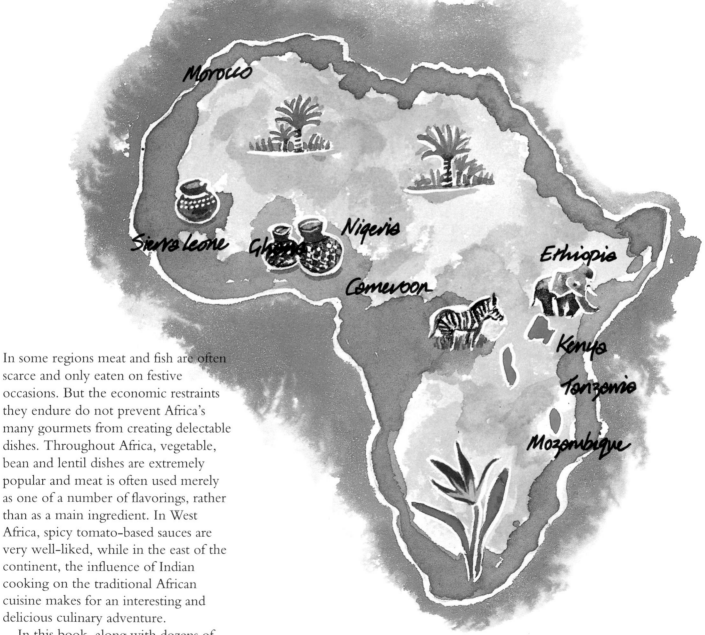

In some regions meat and fish are often scarce and only eaten on festive occasions. But the economic restraints they endure do not prevent Africa's many gourmets from creating delectable dishes. Throughout Africa, vegetable, bean and lentil dishes are extremely popular and meat is often used merely as one of a number of flavorings, rather than as a main ingredient. In West Africa, spicy tomato-based sauces are very well-liked, while in the east of the continent, the influence of Indian cooking on the traditional African cuisine makes for an interesting and delicious culinary adventure.

In this book, along with dozens of colorful and tasty, traditional recipes, such as Joloff Chicken and Rice, there are plenty of variations and adaptations of authentic dishes, such as Kachumbali Salad, as well as several contemporary

dishes, such as Bean and Gari Loaf, and Fish with Red Onions, Lemon and Cilantro, created using traditional ingredients, herbs and spices.

Eating in Africa is a unique and exciting experience, throughout the continent cooks use the same or similar ingredients, but often prepare and cook them in different ways according to local tradition and custom. For example, in some West African countries okra is chopped very finely, until it is reduced almost to a pulp, giving a rich silky consistency to sauces and soups, while elsewhere the okra is often left whole to give a completely different result.

The essential staples - yams, cassava, green bananas and plantains - are used throughout Africa, either on their own or combined with others to make Fu Fu, a popular accompaniment to all sorts of savory dishes.

Sweet potatoes, coconuts, okra, a huge variety of green vegetables, beans and pulses, nuts, and grains, such as corn, are all common cooking ingredients, while all sorts of wonderful, tropical fruits, such as mangoes, avocados and papayas, are a familiar sight and are eaten at any time of the day – not just reserved for dessert.

Two ingredients are worth a particular mention. Chilies add spice and flavor to many dishes, but even adventurous cooks would do well to slowly accustom themselves to the zingingly hot dishes in

Fresh ripe pineapples are in plentiful supply in this bustling fruit market.

which Africans specialize and revel! Less well-known is palm oil, which is unlike any other oil and should be used sparingly – its distinctive, strong flavor is definitely an acquired taste.

This book is largely due to the generosity and enthusiasm of many wonderful women who have welcomed me into their homes to share their culinary skills and treasured secrets. Many of these women had learned recipes from their mothers and grandmothers, others had just acquired a taste and flair for African cooking from visits to the continent. I have traveled to north and west Africa and over the years have also been lucky enough to watch and share with my relatives and friends some of their many glorious meals.

Although you may be unfamiliar

Collecting – and cracking – fresh coconuts is very often a family affair.

with some of the ingredients mentioned in my recipes, you will find that most are available in large supermarkets, street markets, and in particular, African and Asian stores, which often stock a huge variety of fresh fruit and vegetables. If you are not sure about an ingredient, quiz the shop keeper, or even shoppers themselves – I always find that the best way to understand and become familiar with new ingredients is to ask about them.

African cooking is all about being creative and having a feel for the food. My suggestion is to try the recipes, adapt them if you like, and create your own *Taste of Africa*.

INGREDIENTS

ALLSPICE
Available whole or ground, allspice are small, dark brown berries similar in size to large peppercorns. They can be used in sweet or savory dishes and have a flavour of nutmeg, cinnamon and clove, hence the name.

EGGPLANT
In Africa, a yellowish white variety of eggplant is grown, known as a garden egg. These are not widely available in this country but the common purple/black eggplant can be used instead.

BLACK-EYED PEAS
This legume originally came from Africa, where it is a staple food. It can be soaked overnight or boiled without soaking if you allow an extra 1/2 hour. It is used in all sorts of African dishes, soups, stews, rice dishes, salads and snacks. Available in most large supermarkets, delicatessens and health food stores.

Clockwise from top left: Yam, okra, christophene, sweet potatoes.

CILANTRO
Also known as coriander or Chinese parsley, the leaves of this herb look like Italian parsley and add an intense pungent flavor to stews and soups.

CASSAVA
This tropical vegetable has tuberous roots with a brown skin and hard starchy white flesh. Dried and ground, it makes cassava flour and gari (right).

Clockwise from top left: Groundnut oil, palm oil, cashew nuts.

CHILIES
A wide variety of chilies or hot peppers are grown in West Africa. One of the hottest is the fat and fiery Scotch Bonnet. It has a spicy smell and flavor and can be red, green, yellow or brown. Always take care when handling any hot chili as the oils can be very painful if they touch the eyes or any sensitive area. If you don't want very fiery food, remove the seeds and core of chilies, thinly slice and add sparingly to a stew or broth until you know the "heat" you require.

CHAYOTE
This is a pear-shaped vegetable with a cream-colored or green skin. Also known as cho-cho, it has a bland flavor, similar to squash or zucchini.

COCONUT
The flesh and milk of the coconut is used widely in Africa. Coconut milk is available in cans from African and Asian grocers, but make sure to buy the unsweetened variety. Coconut milk can be stored indefinitely. For use in recipes where coconut cream is called for, skim the cream off the top of the milk.

DRIED SHRIMP
These small shrimp are and dried in the sun. They are a popular seasoning in African cuisine and are used to add a distinctive flavor to stews and broths. Available from African, Caribbean and Asian food stores.

EGUSI
This is made from either melon seeds or the seeds of a fruit that is a cross between a gourd and a pumpkin. The seeds are like small almonds and are often ground for recipes. It is available from most African food shops.

FIVE-SPICE POWDER
This reddish-brown powder is a combination of five ground spices – star anise seed, fennel, clove, cinnamon and Szechwan pepper. Use this spice sparingly, it has a wonderful flavor and aroma but can be dominant.

Clockwise from top left: Pomfret, red snapper, tilapia, dried shrimp.

GARI
This is a coarse-ground flour made from cassava and is used in a number of African recipes. It is available from African and Caribbean food shops.

Mangoes – small and large.

Eggplants – large and small – and garden eggs.

GREEN BANANAS

These are unripe bananas, although only certain varieties are used as a green vegetable. They are usually boiled, with or without their skins. A little oil added when boiling helps to keep the saucepan clean. (To peel green bananas, see plantains.)

GROUNDNUT PASTE

Used in West African cooking mainly to make delicious sauces, pure groundnut paste is difficult to find, so substitute natural smooth or crunchy peanut butter. Shelled and skinned roasted peanuts can be ground either with a mortar and pestle or in a spice or coffee grinder.

MANGO

These beautiful fruits, shaped like enormous pips, can be as large as melons or as small as apples. They have a vivid golden flesh with a deep flavor. Green mangoes are used for chutneys and to add tartness to casseroles and stews.

MUNG BEANS

Sometimes known as green gram or golden gram. They are small, bright green dried beans, available from large supermarkets or from Asian or African food stores.

OILS

Palm oil A bright orange/red oil extracted from the fruits of the oil palm. There is really no substitute for palm oil – it gives food a very authentic flavor, but use sparingly, as it can be rather overpowering. Available in most Asian, African or Caribbean food shops.

Groundnut oil Made from peanuts, this is another essential cooking oil if you want to achieve an authentic African flavor. Available from most Asian and African food stores and from large supermarkets.

OKRA

Also known as ladies fingers, these are extremely popular in African cookery and were one of the vegetables taken by the slaves to the Caribbean where they are also widely used. When buying okra, avoid the larger varieties and choose small, firm ones. Wash and dry them *before* topping, tailing and cutting up, this will prevent them from getting too sticky.

PLANTAINS

These members of the banana family can be green, yellow or almost black according to their ripeness. They are inedible raw, but once cooked, either boiled, fried, baked or roasted, have a wonderful flavor. To peel a plantain, remove the top and tail with a sharp knife and cut in half. Make three or four slits lengthwise in the skin without cutting the flesh. Lift off the edge of a slit and run the tip of your thumb under the edge, lengthwise, peeling back and removing all of the skin.

Green bananas and plantains.

Clockwise from top: Gari, black cardamom pods, egusi, melon seeds, mung beans, black-eyed peas.

RED KIDNEY BEANS

All sorts of beans are used in African cookery for casseroles, soups and stews. Red kidney beans are poisonous when raw and should be soaked for several hours or overnight and then boiled rapidly for 10–15 minutes before simmering until tender – they can then be cooked according to the recipe.

SWEET POTATO

The skin of the sweet potato ranges in color from white to pink to reddish brown. There are several varieties, but the white-fleshed, red-skinned variety is most commonly used in African cookery. Sweet potatoes can be boiled, roasted, fried, creamed or baked in their skins – and are ideal for both sweet and savory dishes.

YAM

These come in all sizes – some varieties are huge – so when buying, ask for a piece the size you need. The flesh is either yellow or white and can be eaten boiled, roasted, baked, mashed or made into fries or fu fu.

SOUPS AND APPETIZERS

In some African countries, soup is the whole meal, made using meat or fish, and dried beans or vegetables and served with a staple food such as fu fu, ground rice or boiled yam. One of the most popular soups is Groundnut Soup, made from peanuts, and many African soups are thickened with beans or lentils, while in others the vegetables are chopped so they break up and thicken the broth. Many of the soups in this section have been created using African ingredients and are in the style of soups I came across in my travels. The appetizers can be served as snacks or for light lunches, picnics and parties. They are quick, easy and taste good too.

Lamb and Pumpkin Soup

INGREDIENTS

Serves 4

4 ounces split black-eyed peas, soaked for 1–2 hours, or overnight

1½ pounds shoulder of lamb, cut into medium-size chunks

1 teaspoon chopped fresh thyme, or ½ teaspoon dried

2 bay leaves

5 cups stock or water

1 onion, sliced

8 ounces pumpkin, diced

2 black cardamom pods

1½ teaspoons ground turmeric

1 tablespoon chopped fresh cilantro

½ teaspoon caraway seeds

1 fresh green chili, seeded and chopped

2 green bananas

1 carrot

salt and freshly ground black pepper

1 Drain the black-eyed peas, place them in a saucepan and cover with fresh cold water.

2 Bring the peas to a boil, boil rapidly for 10 minutes and then reduce the heat and simmer, covered, for 40–50 minutes until tender, adding more water if necessary. Remove from the heat and set aside to cool.

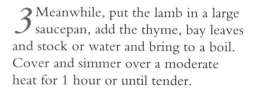

3 Meanwhile, put the lamb in a large saucepan, add the thyme, bay leaves and stock or water and bring to a boil. Cover and simmer over a moderate heat for 1 hour or until tender.

4 Add the onion, pumpkin, cardamom, turmeric, cilantro, caraway, chili and seasoning and stir. Bring back to a simmer and then cook, uncovered, for 15 minutes or until the pumpkin is tender, stirring occasionally.

5 When the peas are cool, spoon into a blender or food processor with their liquid and blend to a smooth purée.

6 Cut the bananas into medium slices and the carrot into thin slices. Stir into the soup with the peas and cook for 10–12 minutes, until the vegetables are tender. Adjust seasoning and serve.

Fish and Okra Soup

The inspiration for this soup came from a Ghanaian recipe for okra soup. Here it is enhanced by the addition of smoked fish.

INGREDIENTS

Serves 4

2 green bananas
4 tablespoons butter or margarine
1 onion, finely chopped
2 tomatoes, peeled and finely chopped
4 ounces okra, trimmed
8 ounces smoked haddock or cod fillet,
 cut into bite-size pieces
3¾ cups fish stock
1 fresh chili, seeded and chopped
salt and freshly ground black pepper
chopped fresh parsley, to garnish

1 Slit the skins of the green bananas and place in a large saucepan. Cover with water, bring to a boil and cook over a moderate heat for about 25 minutes or until the bananas are tender. Transfer to a plate and set aside to cool.

2 Melt the butter or margarine in a large saucepan and sauté the onion for about 5 minutes until soft. Stir in the chopped tomatoes and okra and fry gently for another 10 minutes.

3 Add the fish, fish stock, chili and seasoning, bring to a boil, then reduce the heat and simmer for about 20 minutes or until the fish is cooked through and flakes easily.

4 Peel the cooked bananas and cut into slices. Stir into the soup, heat through for a few minutes and then ladle into soup bowls. Sprinkle with parsley and serve.

Plantain and Corn Soup

INGREDIENTS

Serves 4

2 tablespoons butter or margarine
1 onion, finely chopped
1 garlic clove, crushed
10 ounces yellow plantains, peeled and
    sliced
1 large tomato, peeled and chopped
1 cup corn
1 teaspoon dried tarragon, crushed
3¾ cups vegetable or chicken stock
1 green chili, seeded and chopped
pinch of grated nutmeg
salt and freshly ground black pepper

1 Melt the butter or margarine in a saucepan over a moderate heat, add the onion and garlic and fry for a few minutes until the onion is soft.

2 Add the plantains, tomato and corn and cook for 5 minutes.

3 Add the tarragon, vegetable stock, chili and salt and pepper to taste and simmer for 10 minutes or until the plantain is tender. Stir in the nutmeg and serve at once.

Groundnut Soup

Peanuts, also known as groundnuts, are very widely used in sauces in African cooking. Making a paste with raw peanuts closely approximates the original, but peanut butter is a good substitute. Traditionally the okra are chopped, which gives the soup a slightly "tacky" consistency.

INGREDIENTS

Serves 4

3 tablespoons pure groundnut paste
    or peanut butter
6¼ cups stock or water
2 tablespoons tomato paste
1 onion, chopped
2 slices fresh ginger
¼ teaspoon dried thyme
1 bay leaf
salt and chili powder
8 ounces white yam, diced
10 small okras, trimmed (optional)

1 Place the groundnut paste or peanut butter in a bowl, add 1¼ cups of the stock or water and the tomato paste and blend together to make a smooth paste.

2 Spoon the nut mixture into a saucepan and add the onion, ginger, thyme, bay leaf, salt, chili and the remaining stock.

3 Heat gently until simmering, then cook for 1 hour, stirring from time to time to prevent the nut mixture sticking.

4 Add the white yam, cook for another 10 minutes, and then add the okra, if using, and simmer until both are tender. Serve immediately.

Yam Balls

Yam balls are a popular snack in many African countries. They are traditionally made quite plain, but can be flavored with chopped vegetables and herbs as in this recipe, or with cooked meat or fish, or spices.

INGREDIENTS

Makes about 24 balls
1 pound white yam
2 tablespoons finely chopped onion
3 tablespoons chopped tomatoes
1/2 teaspoon chopped fresh thyme
1 green chili, finely chopped
1 tablespoon finely chopped scallion
1 garlic clove, crushed
1 egg, beaten
salt and freshly ground black pepper
oil, for shallow frying
seasoned flour, for dusting

1 Peel the yam, cut into pieces and boil in salted water for about 30 minutes or until tender. Drain and mash.

2 Add the onion, tomatoes, thyme, chili, scallion, garlic, then stir in the egg and seasoning and mix well.

3 Using a dessert spoon, scoop a little of the mixture at a time and mold into balls. Heat a little oil in a large frying pan, roll the yam balls in the seasoned flour and then fry for a few minutes until golden brown. Drain the yam balls on paper towels and keep them warm while cooking the rest of the mixture. Serve hot.

COOK'S TIP

Add a selection of fresh chopped herbs to the yam mixture; parsley and chives make a good combination. Mix in 2 tablespoons with the egg and seasoning.

Tatale

Overripe plantains are never thrown away and in Ghana they are often used to make this well-loved snack.

INGREDIENTS

Serves 4
2 overripe plantains
2–4 tablespoons self-rising flour
1 small onion, finely chopped
1 egg, beaten
1 teaspoon palm oil (optional)
salt
1 fresh green chili, seeded and chopped
oil, for shallow frying

1 Peel and mash the plantains. Place in bowl and add enough flour to bind, stirring thoroughly.

2 Add the onion, egg, palm oil, if using, salt and chili. Mix well and let stand for 20 minutes.

3 Heat a little oil in a large frying pan. Spoon dessert spoons of the mixture into the pan and fry in batches for 3–4 minutes until golden, turning once. Drain the fritters on paper towels and serve hot or cold.

Spicy Kebabs

INGREDIENTS

Makes 18–20 balls
1 pound ground beef
1 egg
3 garlic cloves, crushed
½ onion, finely chopped
½ teaspoon freshly ground black pepper
1½ teaspoons ground cumin
1½ teaspoons dhania (ground coriander)
1 teaspoon ground ginger
2 teaspoons garam masala
1 tablespoon lemon juice
1–1½ cups fresh white bread crumbs
1 small chili, seeded and chopped
salt
oil, for deep frying
Kachumbali or spicy dip, to serve

1 Place the ground beef in a large bowl and add the egg, garlic, onion, spices, seasoning, lemon juice, about 1 cup of the bread crumbs and the chili.

2 Using your hands or a wooden spoon, mix the ingredients together until the mixture is firm. If it feels sticky, add more of the bread crumbs and mix again until firm.

3 Heat the oil in a large heavy pan or deep-fat fryer. Shape the mixture into balls or fingers and fry, a few at a time, for 5 minutes or until well browned all over.

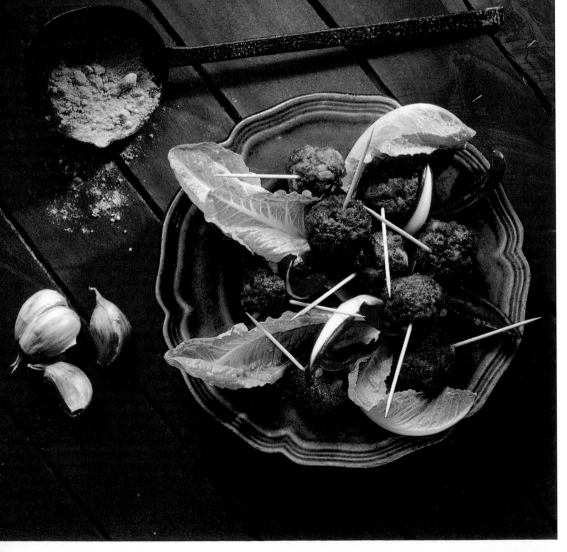

4 Using a slotted spoon, drain the kebabs and then transfer to a plate lined with paper towels. Cook the remaining kebabs in the same way and then serve, if you like, with Kachumbali or a spicy dip.

Assortment of Plantains

This melange of succulent sweet and savory plantains makes a delicious crunchy appetizer.

INGREDIENTS

Serves 4
2 green plantains
1 yellow plantain
½ onion
pinch of garlic powder
salt and cayenne pepper
vegetable oil, for shallow frying

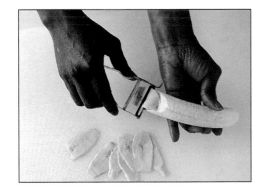

1 Heat the oil in a large frying pan over a moderate heat. While the oil is heating, peel one of the green plantains and cut into very thin rounds, using a vegetable peeler.

2 Fry the plantain rounds in the oil for about 3 minutes, turning, until golden brown. Drain on paper towels and keep warm.

3 Coarsely grate the other green plantain and put on a plate. Slice the onion into wafer-thin shreds and mix with the grated plantain.

4 Heat a little more oil in the frying pan and fry handfuls of the mixture for 2–3 minutes, until golden, turning once. Drain on paper towels and keep warm with the green plantain rounds.

5 Heat a little more oil in the frying pan and, while it is heating, peel the yellow plantain, cut in half lengthwise and dice. Sprinkle with garlic powder and cayenne pepper and then fry in the hot oil until golden brown, turning to brown evenly. Drain on paper towels and then arrange the three varieties of cooked plantains in shallow dishes. Sprinkle with salt and serve as·a snack.

Cameroon Suya

INGREDIENTS

Serves 4

1 pound round or flank steak
½ teaspoon sugar
1 teaspoon garlic powder
1 teaspoon ground ginger
1 teaspoon paprika
1 teaspoon ground cinnamon
pinch of chili powder
2 teaspoons onion salt
½ cup peanuts, finely crushed
vegetable oil, for brushing

2 Mix the sugar, garlic powder, spices and onion salt together in a small bowl. Add the crushed peanuts, then add this mixture to the steak, mixing well so that the spices are worked into the meat.

3 Thread the steak on to six satay sticks, pushing the meat close together. Place in a shallow dish, cover loosely with foil and let marinate in a cool place for a few hours.

4 Preheat a broiler or barbecue grill. Brush the meat with a little oil and then cook over a moderate heat for about 15 minutes, until evenly brown.

1 Trim the steak of any fat and then cut into 1-inch wide strips. Place in a bowl or a shallow dish.

COOK'S TIP

If barbecueing the meat, try to avoid it cooking too quickly or burning.

Akkras

These tasty fritters, are almost always made from black-eyed peas. For a quicker version: after soaking the peas, drain and purée without removing the skins.

INGREDIENTS

Serves 4

1¼ cups dried black-eyed peas
1 onion, chopped
1 red chili, halved, with seeds removed (optional)
⅔ cup water
oil, for deep frying

1 Soak the black-eyed peas in plenty of cold water for 6–8 hours or overnight. Drain the beans and then, with a brisk action, rub the beans between the palms of your hands to remove the skins.

2 Return the beans to the bowl, cover with water and the skins will float to the surface. Discard the skins and soak the beans again for 2 hours.

3 Place the beans in a blender or food processor with the onion, chili, if using, and a little water. Blend to make a thick paste. Pour the mixture into a large bowl and whisk for a few minutes.

4 Heat the oil in a large heavy saucepan and fry spoonfuls of the mixture for 4 minutes until golden brown.

Avocado and Smoked Fish Salad

Avocado and smoked fish make a good combination and, flavored with herbs and spices, create a delectable salad.

INGREDIENTS

Serves 4

1 tablespoon butter or margarine
½ onion, finely sliced
1 teaspoon white mustard seeds
8 ounces smoked mackerel, flaked
2 tablespoons cilantro leaves, chopped
2 firm tomatoes, peeled and chopped
1 tablespoon lemon juice

For the salad

2 avocados
½ cucumber
1 tablespoon lemon juice
2 firm tomatoes
1 green chili
salt and freshly ground black pepper

1 Melt the butter or margarine in a frying pan, add the onion and mustard seeds and fry for about 5 minutes or until the onion is soft.

2 Add the fish, cilantro leaves, tomatoes and lemon juice and cook over a low heat for 2–3 minutes. Remove from the heat and cool.

3 To make the salad, slice the avocados and cucumber thinly. Place together in a bowl and sprinkle with the lemon juice.

4 Slice and seed the tomatoes and finely chop the chili.

5 Place the fish mixture in the center of a large serving plate.

6 Arrange the avocados, cucumber and tomatoes decoratively around the fish. Alternatively, spoon a quarter of the fish mixture on to each of four serving plates and divide the avocados, cucumber and tomatoes equally among them. Sprinkle with the chopped chili and a little salt and pepper and serve.

--- COOK'S TIP ---

Smoked mackerel has a distinctive flavor, but cooked smoked haddock or cod can also be used in this salad, or try a mixture. For a speedy variation, canned tuna makes a convenient substitute.

Jumbo Shrimp with Spicy Salsa

The spicy salsa served with this dish is equally good made from peanuts instead of cashew nuts. Vegetarians can enjoy this, too, if you make it with vegetables or tofu cubes. For a light meal, serve with boiled rice or bread.

INGREDIENTS

Serves 4–6
24 unshelled raw jumbo shrimp
juice of ½ lemon
1 teaspoon paprika
1 bay leaf
1 thyme sprig
salt and freshly ground black pepper
vegetable oil, for brushing

For the spicy salsa
1 onion, chopped
4 canned plum tomatoes, plus
   4 tablespoons of the juice
½ green bell pepper, seeded and chopped
1 garlic clove, crushed
1 tablespoon cashew nuts
1 tablespoon soy sauce
1 tablespoon dried coconut

1 Shell the shrimp, leaving the tails on. Place in a shallow dish and sprinkle with the lemon juice, paprika and seasoning. Cover and chill.

2 Put the shells in a saucepan with the bay leaf and thyme, cover with water, and bring to a boil. Simmer for about 30 minutes, then strain the stock into a 2-cup measure. Top up with water, if necessary, to 1¼ cups.

3 To make the spicy salsa, place all the ingredients in a blender or food processor and blend until smooth.

4 Pour into a saucepan with the shrimp stock and simmer over a moderate heat for 30 minutes or until the sauce is fairly thick.

5 Preheat a broiler. Thread the shrimp onto small skewers, then brush the shrimp on both sides with a little oil and broil under a low heat until cooked, turning once. Serve the shrimp with the salsa for an hors d'oeuvres. For a main course, omit the skewers, broil the shrimp and pour the sauce over them.

COOK'S TIP

If unshelled raw shrimp are not available, use cooked jumbo shrimp instead. Just broil for a short time, until they are completely heated through.

MEAT AND POULTRY

With recipes from Ethiopia, Ghana, Tanzania, Nigeria, Kenya and Cameroon, there is something for everyone in this section. Meat is usually cooked in spicy sauces, and frequently is flavored with smoked fish or dried shrimp. Hot chilies add a really fiery flavor to many of our dishes and I suggest you use them carefully to begin with, until you know how much you and your friends and guests like. Chicken and other poultry like duck and turkey are also cooked with vegetables and beans, herbs and spices. Meat and poultry would be served with a selection of side dishes, usually a starchy vegetable like yam, green bananas, plantain or with fu fu, rice or breads.

Nigerian Meat Stew

This recipe was adapted from a Nigerian stew, originally made with meats of different flavors, such as beef, liver and mutton, along with dried fish or snails, and served with yam or rice.

INGREDIENTS

Serves 4–6

1½ pounds oxtail, chopped
1 pound stewing beef, cubed
1 pound skinless, boneless chicken
    breasts, chopped
2 garlic cloves, crushed
1½ onions
2 tablespoons palm or vegetable oil
2 tablespoons tomato paste
14-ounce can plum tomatoes
2 bay leaves
1 teaspoon dried thyme
1 teaspoon allspice
salt and freshly ground black pepper

1 Place the oxtail in a large saucepan, cover with water and bring to a boil. Skim the surface of any froth, then cover and cook for 1½ hours, adding more water as necessary.

2 Add the beef and continue to cook for another hour or until tender.

3 Meanwhile, season the chicken with the crushed garlic and coarsely chop one of the onions.

4 Heat the oil in a large saucepan over a moderate heat and fry the chopped onion for about 5 minutes until soft. Stir in the tomato paste, cook briskly for a few minutes, then add the chicken. Stir well and cook gently for 5 minutes.

5 Meanwhile, place the plum tomatoes and the remaining half onion in a food processor and blend to a purée. Stir into the chicken mixture with the bay leaves, thyme, allspice and seasoning.

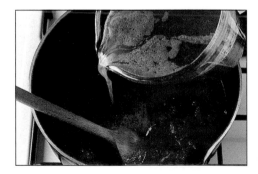

6 Add about 2½ cups of stock from the cooked oxtail and beef and simmer for 35 minutes.

7 Add the oxtail and beef to the chicken. Heat gently, adjust the seasoning and serve hot.

Kofta Curry

Although fussy to make, these koftas are well worth it. To save time, prepare in advance and chill until ready to cook.

INGREDIENTS

Serves 4

1 pound ground beef or lamb
3 tablespoons finely chopped onion
1 tablespoon chopped fresh cilantro
1 tablespoon plain yogurt
about 4 tablespoons flour
2 teaspoons ground cumin
1 teaspoon garam masala
1 teaspoon ground turmeric
1 teaspoon dhania (ground coriander)
1 green chili, seeded and finely chopped
2 garlic cloves, crushed
¼ teaspoon black mustard seeds
1 egg (optional)
salt and freshly ground black pepper

For the curry sauce

2 tablespoons ghee or butter
1 onion, finely chopped
2 garlic cloves, crushed
3 tablespoons curry powder
4 green cardamom pods
2½ cups hot chicken stock or water
1 tablespoon tomato paste
2 tablespoons plain yogurt
1 tablespoon chopped fresh cilantro

1 Put the ground beef or lamb into a large bowl, add all the remaining meatball ingredients and mix well with your hands. Roll the mixture into small balls and put aside on a floured plate until required.

2 To make the curry sauce, heat the ghee or butter in a saucepan over a moderate heat and fry the onion and garlic for about 10 minutes until the onion is soft and buttery.

3 Reduce the heat and then add the curry powder and cardamon pods and cook for a few minutes, stirring well.

4 Slowly stir in the stock or water, and then add the tomato paste, yogurt and cilantro and stir well.

5 Simmer gently for 10 minutes. Add the koftas a few at a time, allow to cook briefly and then add a few more, until all of the koftas are in the pan. Simmer, uncovered, for about 20 minutes or until the koftas are cooked through. Avoid stirring, but gently shake the pan occasionally to move the koftas around. The curry should thicken slightly but if it becomes too dry, add a little more stock or water. Serve hot.

COOK'S TIP

Ghee is an East Indian form of clarified or drawn butter that can be heated to high temperatures without burning. It keeps for 6 months in a refrigerator. Ghee is widely used in Indian and Pakistani cooking and, because it is pre-cooked, has a distinctive, slightly nutty, flavor.

Lamb and Vegetable Pilaf

INGREDIENTS

Serves 4

For the meat curry

1-pound boned shoulder of lamb, cubed
½ teaspoon dried thyme
½ teaspoon paprika
1 teaspoon garam masala
1 garlic clove, crushed
1½ tablespoons vegetable oil
3¾ cups lamb stock or water
salt and freshly ground black pepper

For the rice

2 tablespoons butter or margarine
1 onion, chopped
6 ounces potato, diced
1 carrot, sliced
½ red bell pepper, seeded and chopped
4 ounces green cabbage, sliced
1 green chili, seeded and finely chopped
4 tablespoons plain yogurt
½ teaspoon ground cumin
5 green cardamom pods
2 garlic cloves, crushed
1½ cups basmati rice
about ½ cup cashew nuts
salt and freshly ground black pepper

1 First make the meat curry. Place the lamb in a large bowl and add the thyme, paprika, garam masala, garlic and salt and pepper. Stir well to mix, then cover and set aside in a cool place for 2–3 hours to marinate.

2 Heat the oil in a large saucepan and fry the lamb, in batches if necessary, over a moderate heat for 5–6 minutes, until browned.

3 Add the stock or water, stir well and then cook, covered, for 35–40 minutes or until the lamb is just tender. Transfer the lamb to a plate or bowl and pour the liquid into a 3-cup measure, adding water if necessary, to make 2½ cups.

4 To make the rice, melt the butter or margarine and fry the onion, potato and carrot for 5 minutes.

5 Add the red pepper, cabbage, chili, yogurt, spices, garlic and the reserved meat stock. Stir well, cover, and then simmer gently for 5–10 minutes, until the cabbage has wilted.

6 Stir in the rice and lamb, cover and simmer over a low heat for 20 minutes or until the rice is cooked. Sprinkle in the cashew nuts and season to taste with salt and freshly ground black pepper. Serve hot.

COOK'S TIP

If you prefer, fewer vegetables can be used for this dish and cubed chicken or ground lamb substituted for the cubed lamb. Basmati rice is ideal, but long grain rice may be used instead. The amount of liquid can be varied, depending on whether firm or well-cooked rice is preferred.

Spiced Fried Lamb

An Ethiopian dish, *Awaze Tibs*, is flavored with a red pepper spice mixture called *berbiri*, which is traditionally made from a variety of East African herbs and spices. This version uses spices that are a little easier to find!

INGREDIENTS

Serves 4

1 pound lamb loin
3 tablespoons olive oil
1 red onion, sliced
½ teaspoon grated fresh ginger
2 garlic cloves, crushed
½ green chili, seeded and finely chopped (optional)
1 tablespoon clarified butter or ghee
salt and freshly ground black pepper

For the berbiri

½ teaspoon each chili powder, paprika, ground ginger, ground cinnamon, ground cardamom seeds and dried basil
1 teaspoon garlic powder

1 To make the berbiri, combine all the ingredients in a small bowl and tip into an airtight container. Berberi will keep for several months if stored in a dry cool place.

2 Trim the meat of any fat and then cut into ¾-inch cubes.

3 Heat the oil in a large frying pan and fry the meat and onion for 5–6 minutes, until the meat is browned on all sides.

4 Add the ginger and garlic to the pan with 2 teaspoons of the berbiri, then stir-fry over a brisk heat for another 5–10 minutes.

5 Add the chili, if using, and season well with salt and pepper. Just before serving, add the butter or ghee and stir well.

COOK'S TIP

Clarified butter is traditionally used for this recipe. It can be made by gently heating butter (preferably sweet) up to boiling point, and then scooping off the milk solids that rise to the surface.

Lamb Tagine with Cilantro and Spices

This Moroccan-style stew can be made with chops or cutlets and either marinated for a few hours before cooking or cooked immediately after seasoning.

INGREDIENTS

Serves 4
4 lamb chops or cutlets
2 garlic cloves, crushed
pinch of saffron strands
½ teaspoon ground cinnamon, plus extra to garnish
½ teaspoon ground ginger
1 tablespoon chopped fresh cilantro
1 tablespoon chopped fresh parsley
1 onion, finely chopped
3 tablespoons olive oil
1¼ cups lamb stock
½ cup blanched almonds, to garnish
1 teaspoon sugar
salt and freshly ground black pepper

1 Season the lamb with the garlic, saffron, cinnamon, ginger and a little salt and black pepper. Place on a large plate and sprinkle with the cilantro, parsley and onion. Cover loosely and set aside in the fridge for a few hours to marinate.

2 Heat the oil in a large frying pan, over a moderate heat. Add the marinated lamb and all the herbs and onion from the dish.

3 Fry for 1–2 minutes, turning once, then add the stock, bring to a boil and simmer gently for 30 minutes, turning the chops once.

4 Meanwhile, heat a small frying pan over a moderate heat, add the almonds and dry fry until golden, shaking the pan occasionally to make sure they color evenly. Transfer to a bowl and set aside.

5 Transfer the chops to a serving plate and keep warm. Increase the heat under the pan and boil the sauce until reduced by about half. Stir in the sugar. Pour the sauce over the chops and sprinkle with the fried almonds and a little extra ground cinnamon.

COOK'S TIP

Lamb tagine is a fragrant dish, originating in North Africa. It is traditionally made in a cooking dish known as a tagine, from which it takes its name. This dish consists of a shallow pot with a conical lid. It has a narrow opening to let steam escape, while retaining the flavor.

Roast Lamb with Saffron and Tomato

A favorite roast for Sunday lunch. Boiled rice, root vegetables and fried plantain make delicious accompaniments.

INGREDIENTS

Serves 6

2 garlic cloves, crushed
1 tablespoon finely chopped fresh mint
2 teaspoons ground cumin
1 teaspoon dried thyme
3 tablespoons lemon juice
2 tablespoons olive oil
3-pound leg of lamb
lamb stock, for basting (optional)
salt and freshly ground black pepper

For the saffron and tomato sauce

2 tablespoons vegetable oil
1 red onion, sliced
2 garlic cloves, crushed
14-ounce can chopped tomatoes
2 teaspoons ground cinnamon
1 teaspoon dried tarragon
generous pinch of saffron threads
4 slices fresh ginger
1 green chili, seeded and finely
  chopped
2½ cups lamb stock or water
salt and freshly ground black pepper

COOK'S TIP

African cooks almost always prefer to roast lamb until it is well done. If you prefer it a little pinker, then reduce the cooking time accordingly.

1 Mix together the garlic, mint, cumin, thyme, lemon juice, olive oil and salt and pepper. Cut three fairly deep slits into the lamb and rub the mixture all over the meat, pressing well into the slits. Cover loosely with plastic wrap and leave to marinate overnight in the fridge.

2 Preheat the oven to 375°F. Place the lamb in a large roasting pan, cover with foil and roast for about 2 hours, basting occasionally with the pan juices or a little stock, if preferred.

3 Meanwhile make the sauce, heat the oil in a large saucepan and fry the onion and garlic over a moderate heat for 4–5 minutes until the onion is fairly soft.

4 Add the tomatoes, cinnamon, tarragon, saffron, ginger, chili and seasoning. Stir well and cook, uncovered, for about 5 minutes.

5 Add the stock or water, bring back to a boil and then simmer for about 30 minutes until well reduced and fairly thick. Adjust the seasoning if necessary and then remove the pan from the heat.

6 Transfer the cooked lamb to a serving plate, cover with foil and let stand in a warm place for 5–10 minutes. Pour off the excess fat from the roasting pan, then add the meat juices to the sauce and reheat. Carve the lamb into thin slices and serve with the sauce, accompanied by thick slices of fried plantain.

VARIATIONS

Saffron is expensive, but you can use turmeric as a substitute to give a golden yellow color. A lean cut shoulder of lamb can be used instead of the leg of lamb.

East African Roast Chicken

INGREDIENTS

Serves 6

4–4¹⁄₂-pound chicken
2 tablespoons softened butter, plus
  extra for basting
3 garlic cloves, crushed
1 teaspoon freshly ground black pepper
1 teaspoon ground turmeric
¹⁄₂ teaspoon ground cumin
1 teaspoon dried thyme
1 tablespoon finely chopped fresh
  cilantro
4 tablespoons thick coconut milk
4 tablespoons medium-dry sherry
1 teaspoon tomato paste
salt and chili powder

1 Remove the giblets from the chicken, if necessary, rinse out the cavity and pat the skin dry.

2 Put the butter and all the remaining ingredients in a bowl and mix together well to form a thick paste.

3 Gently ease the skin of the chicken away from the flesh and rub generously with the herb and butter mixture. Rub more of the mixture over the skin, legs and wings of the chicken and into the neck cavity.

4 Place the chicken in a roasting pan, cover loosely with foil and marinate overnight in the fridge.

5 Preheat the oven to 375°F. Cover the chicken with clean foil and roast for 1 hour, then turn the chicken over and baste with the pan juices. Cover again with foil and cook for 30 minutes.

6 Remove the foil and place the chicken breast-side up. Rub with a little extra butter and roast for a further 10–15 minutes or until the meat juices run clear and the skin is golden brown. Serve with a rice dish or a salad.

Yassa Chicken

Senegalese cooks make wonderful Yassa. Instead of frying, they often broil the chicken before adding it to the sauce. For a less tangy flavor, you can add less lemon juice, although it does mellow after cooking.

INGREDIENTS

Serves 4

²⁄₃ cup lemon juice
4 tablespoons malt vinegar
3 onions, sliced
4 tablespoons peanut or vegetable oil
2¹⁄₄ pounds chicken pieces
1 thyme sprig
1 green chili, seeded and finely chopped
2 bay leaves
1⁷⁄₈ cups chicken stock

1 Mix the lemon juice, vinegar, onions and 2 tablespoons of the oil, place the chicken pieces in a shallow dish and pour over the lemon mixture. Cover with plastic wrap and let marinate for 3 hours.

2 Heat the remaining oil in a large saucepan and fry the chicken pieces for 4–5 minutes until browned.

3 Add the marinated onions to the chicken. Fry for 3 minutes, then add the marinade, thyme, chili, bay leaves and half the stock.

4 Cover the pan and simmer gently over a moderate heat for about 35 minutes, until the chicken is cooked through, adding more stock as the sauce evaporates. Serve hot.

Joloff Chicken and Rice

Serve this well-known, colorful West African dish at a dinner party or other special occasion.

Ingredients

Serves 4

2¼-pound chicken, cut into 4–6 pieces
2 garlic cloves, crushed
1 teaspoon dried thyme
2 tablespoons palm or vegetable oil
14-ounce can chopped tomatoes
1 tablespoon tomato paste
1 onion, chopped
1⅞ cups chicken stock or water
2 tablespoons dried shrimp or crayfish, ground
1 green chili, seeded and finely chopped
1½ cups long grain rice, washed

1 Rub the chicken with the garlic and thyme and set aside.

2 Heat the oil in a saucepan until hot but not smoking and then add the chopped tomatoes, tomato paste and onion. Cook over a moderately high heat for about 15 minutes, until the tomatoes are well reduced, stirring occasionally at first and then more frequently as the tomatoes thicken.

3 Reduce the heat a little, add the chicken pieces and stir well to coat with the sauce. Cook for 10 minutes, stirring, then add the stock or water, the dried shrimp or crayfish and the chili. Bring to a boil and simmer for 5 minutes, stirring occasionally.

4 Put the rice in a separate saucepan. Scoop 1¼ cups of the sauce into a 2-cup measure, add water to make up to 1⅞ cups and stir into the rice.

5 Cook, covered, until the liquid is absorbed, place a piece of foil on top of the rice, cover the pan with a lid and cook over a low heat for 20 minutes until the rice is cooked, adding a little more water if necessary.

6 Transfer the chicken pieces to a warmed serving plate. Simmer the sauce until reduced by half. Pour over the chicken and serve with the rice.

Chicken with Lentils

Kuku, this delicious tangy chicken stew, comes from Kenya. The amount of lemon juice can be reduced, if you would prefer a less sharp sauce.

INGREDIENTS

Serves 4–6
6 chicken thighs or pieces
½–¾ teaspoon ground ginger
2 ounces mung beans
4 tablespoons corn oil
2 onions, fincly chopped
2 garlic cloves, crushed
5 tomatoes, peeled and chopped
1 green chili, seeded and finely
  chopped
2 tablespoons lemon juice
1¼ cups coconut milk
1¼ cups water
1 tablespoon chopped fresh cilantro
salt and freshly ground black pepper

1 Season the chicken pieces with the ginger and a little salt and pepper and set aside in a cool place to marinate. Meanwhile, boil the mung beans in plenty of water for 35 minutes until soft, drain, and then mash well.

2 Heat the oil in a large saucepan over a moderate heat and fry the chicken pieces, in batches if necessary, until evenly browned. Transfer to a plate and set aside, reserving the oil and chicken juices in the pan.

3 In the same pan, fry the onions and garlic for 5 minutes, then add the tomatoes and chili and cook for another 1–2 minutes, stirring well.

4 Add the mashed mung beans, lemon juice and coconut milk to the pan. Simmer for 5 minutes, then add the chicken pieces and a little water, if the sauce is too thick. Stir in the cilantro and simmer for about 35 minutes or until the chicken is cooked through. Serve with a green vegetable and rice or chappatis.

Palava Chicken

This is a variation of the popular sauce from Ghana, which was originally made from fish. In Sierra Leone, peanut butter is often added, as in this version.

INGREDIENTS

Serves 4–6

1½ pounds skinless, boneless chicken breasts
2 garlic cloves, crushed
2 tablespoons butter or margarine
2 tablespoons palm or vegetable oil
1 onion, finely chopped
4 tomatoes, peeled and chopped
2 tablespoons peanut butter
2½ cups chicken stock or water
1 thyme sprig or 1 teaspoon dried thyme
8 ounces frozen leaf spinach, defrosted and chopped
1 fresh chili, seeded and chopped
salt and freshly ground black pepper

1 Cut the chicken breasts into thin slices, place in a bowl and stir in the garlic and a little salt and pepper. Melt the butter or margarine in a large frying pan and fry the chicken over a moderate heat, turning once or twice to brown evenly. Transfer to a plate with a slotted spoon and set aside.

2 Heat the oil in a large saucepan and fry the onion and tomatoes over a high heat for 5 minutes until soft.

3 Reduce the heat, add the peanut butter and half of the stock or water and blend together well.

4 Cook for 4–5 minutes, stirring constantly to prevent the peanut butter burning, then add the remaining stock or water, thyme, spinach, chili and seasoning. Stir in the chicken slices and cook over a moderate heat for about 10–15 minutes or until the chicken is cooked through.

5 Pour into a warmed serving dish and serve with boiled yams, rice or ground rice.

COOK'S TIP

If you're short of time, frozen spinach is more convenient, but chopped fresh spinach adds a fresher flavor to this recipe. Egusi (ground melon seed) can be used instead of peanut butter.

Duck with Sherry and Pumpkin

INGREDIENTS

Serves 6

1 whole duck, about 4–4½ pounds
1 lemon
1 teaspoon garlic powder or 2 garlic
  cloves, crushed
1 teaspoon curry powder
½ teaspoon paprika
¾ teaspoon five-spice powder
2 tablespoons soy sauce
salt and freshly ground black pepper
vegetable oil, for frying

For the sauce

3 ounces pumpkin
1 onion, chopped
4 canned plum tomatoes
1¼ cups medium-dry sherry
1¼ cups water

1 Cut the duck into ten pieces and place in a large bowl. Halve the lemon and squeeze the juice all over the duck and set aside.

2 In a small bowl, mix together the garlic, curry powder, paprika, five-spice powder and salt and pepper and rub into each of the duck pieces.

3 Sprinkle the duck with the soy sauce, cover loosely with plastic wrap and let marinate overnight.

4 To make the sauce, cook the pumpkin in boiling water until tender, then blend to a purée with the onion and tomatoes.

--- COOK'S TIP ---

The back and wings of the duck are rather bony, so try and use just the fleshier parts or buy leg or breast portions.

5 Pat the duck pieces dry with paper towels, then heat a little oil in a wok or large frying pan and fry the duck for 15 minutes or until crisp and brown. Set aside on a plate.

6 Wipe off the excess oil from the wok or frying pan with paper towels and pour in the pumpkin purée. Add the sherry and a little of the water, then bring to a boil and add the fried duck. Simmer for about 1 hour or until the duck is cooked, adding more water if the sauce becomes too thick. Serve hot and pass soy sauce separately.

Stuffed Turkey Fillets in Lemon Sauce

Sweet potatoes and shrimp flavored with herbs and chili make an unusual stuffing for turkey fillets. Reduce the amount of fresh chili, if you prefer your food less hot.

INGREDIENTS

Serves 4

6 ounces sweet potato
1 onion, finely chopped
1 teaspoon dried tarragon, crushed
½ teaspoon dried basil
1 green chili, seeded and finely chopped
1 garlic clove, crushed
½ teaspoon dried thyme
½ teaspoon freshly ground black pepper
4 ounces cooked, peeled shrimp, chopped
4 turkey fillets, about 8 ounces each
salt and freshly ground black pepper

For the lemon sauce
1 tablespoon olive oil
½ onion, finely chopped
2 garlic cloves, crushed
1¼ cups well-flavored chicken stock or canned broth
¾ teaspoon dried thyme
½ teaspoon dried basil
2 tablespoons finely chopped fresh parsley
freshly ground black pepper
2 tablespoons lemon juice

1 Preheat the oven to 350°F. Cook the sweet potato in boiling water until tender, then drain, transfer to a bowl and mash to a purée.

2 Add the onion, tarragon, basil, chili, garlic clove, thyme, black pepper and shrimp and mix well.

COOK'S TIP

If you prefer smaller fillets, use chicken instead of turkey, and reduce the cooking time in the oven by about half.

3 Lay the turkey fillets on a plate and season with salt and little extra black pepper. Place a little of the sweet potato stuffing in the center of each fillet, fold over the sides and roll up. Secure with a wooden toothpick, if necessary, and place in a buttered ovenproof dish, seam-side down.

4 To make the lemon sauce, heat the olive oil in a frying pan over a moderate heat and fry the onion and garlic for 5–7 minutes, until soft, stirring frequently. Stir in the stock and simmer for a few minutes.

5 Stir in the thyme, basil, parsley, pepper and lemon juice and simmer for 2 minutes, then pour the sauce around the turkey, cover with foil and bake in the oven for about 1½ hours or until the turkey is cooked, basting frequently with the sauce to keep the rolls moist. Serve with root vegetables, bulgur or rice.

FISH AND SEAFOOD

African waters are teeming with interesting and tasty fish and shellfish – from the humble mackerel to the fabulous lobster. There are more than 200 types of fish in Nigeria alone! For those who live around the coast or by lakes or rivers, fresh fish can be found in abundance and there are a huge number of superb fish dishes, like Fish and Shrimp with Spinach and Coconut, and Fish with Crabmeat and Eggplant, which have been adapted to use fish easily available in this country. Other recipes, like Tanzanian Fish Curry, or Baked Red Snapper, use fish that are increasingly available in larger supermarkets, and are well worth looking out for.

Fish with Crabmeat and Eggplant

Any filleted white fish can be used in this dish in place of the salmon – cod, haddock or halibut would all make good substitutes. For a change, use shelled shrimp instead of the crabmeat.

INGREDIENTS

Serves 4
1–1½ pounds salmon fillet, skinned and cut into 4 pieces
2 garlic cloves, crushed
juice of ½ lemon
1 tablespoon vegetable oil
1 tablespoon butter or margarine
1 onion, cut into rings
6 ounces fresh or canned crabmeat
salt and freshly ground black pepper

For the eggplant sauce
2 tablespoons butter or margarine
2 tablespoons chopped scallion
2 tomatoes, peeled and chopped
½ red bell pepper, seeded and chopped
1 large eggplant, peeled and chopped
1⅞ cups fish or vegetable stock or stock cube and water
salt and freshly ground black pepper

1 Place the salmon fillet in a shallow dish, season with the garlic and a little salt and pepper. Sprinkle with the lemon juice and set aside, covered, to marinate for at least 1 hour.

2 Meanwhile, make the eggplant sauce. Melt the butter or margarine in a saucepan and gently fry the scallion and tomatoes for 5 minutes.

3 Add the red pepper and eggplant, stir together and then add 1¼ cups of the stock. Simmer for 20 minutes until the eggplant is mushy and the liquid has been absorbed, and then mash together well with a fork.

4 To cook the salmon, heat the oil and butter or margarine in a large frying pan. When the butter has melted, sprinkle the onion rings over the bottom of the pan and lay the salmon pieces on top. Cover each piece of salmon with crabmeat and then spoon the eggplant mixture on top.

5 Pour the remaining stock around the salmon, cover with a lid and cook over a low to moderate heat until the salmon is cooked through and flakes easily when tested with a knife. The sauce should be thick and fairly dry.

6 Arrange the fish on warmed serving plates, spoon extra sauce over and serve at once.

--- COOK'S TIP ---

Use a spatula to carefully transfer the salmon fillet to serving plates, to prevent breaking up the fish.

Baked Red Snapper

INGREDIENTS

Serves 3–4

1 large red snapper, about 1½–2 pounds cleaned
juice of 1 lemon
½ teaspoon paprika
½ teaspoon garlic powder
½ teaspoon dried thyme
½ teaspoon freshly ground black pepper

For the sauce

2 tablespoons palm or vegetable oil
1 onion
14-ounce can chopped tomatoes
2 garlic cloves
1 thyme sprig or ½ teaspoon dried thyme
1 green chili, seeded and finely chopped
½ green bell pepper, seeded and chopped
1¼ cups fish stock or water

1 Preheat the oven to 400°F and then prepare the sauce. Heat the oil in a saucepan, fry the onion for 5 minutes, then add the tomatoes, garlic, thyme and chili.

COOK'S TIP

If you prefer less sauce, remove the foil after 20 minutes and continue baking uncovered, until cooked.

2 Add the pepper and stock or water. Bring to a boil, stirring, then reduce the heat and simmer, covered, for about 10 minutes until the vegetables are soft. Leave to cool a little and then place in a blender or food processor and blend to a purée.

3 Wash the fish well and then score the skin with a sharp knife in a criss-cross pattern. Mix together the lemon juice, paprika, garlic, thyme and black pepper, spoon over the fish and rub in well.

4 Place the fish in a greased baking pan and pour the sauce over the top. Cover with foil and bake for about 30–40 minutes or until the fish is cooked and flakes easily when tested with a fork. Serve with boiled rice.

Fish with Lemon, Red Onions and Cilantro

INGREDIENTS

Serves 4

4 halibut or cod steaks or fillets, about
   6 ounces each
juice of 1 lemon
1 teaspoon garlic powder
1 teaspoon paprika
1 teaspoon ground cumin
¾ teaspoon dried tarragon
4 tablespoons olive oil
flour, for dusting
1¼ cups fish stock
2 red chilies, seeded and finely chopped
2 tablespoons chopped fresh cilantro
1 red onion, cut into rings
salt and freshly ground black pepper

1 Place the fish in a shallow bowl and mix together the lemon juice, garlic, paprika, cumin, tarragon and a little salt and pepper. Spoon over the lemon mixture, cover loosely with plastic wrap and allow to marinate for a few hours or overnight in the fridge.

2 Gently heat all of the oil in a large nonstick frying pan, dust the fish with flour and then fry the fish for a few minutes on each side, until golden brown all over.

3 Pour the fish stock around the fish, and simmer, covered, for about 5 minutes or until the fish is thoroughly cooked through.

4 Add the chopped red chilies and 1 tablespoon of the cilantro to the pan. Simmer for 5 minutes.

5 Transfer the fish and sauce to a serving plate and keep warm.

6 Wipe out the pan, add and heat some olive oil and stir fry the onion rings until speckled brown. Sprinkle over the fish with the remaining chopped cilantro and serve at once.

Jumbo Shrimp in Almond Sauce

INGREDIENTS

Serves 4

1 pound raw jumbo shrimp
2½ cups water
3 thin slices fresh ginger
2 teaspoons curry powder
2 garlic cloves, crushed
1 tablespoon butter or margarine
4 tablespoons ground almonds
1 green chili, seeded and finely
  chopped
3 tablespoons light cream
salt and freshly ground black pepper

For the vegetables

1 tablespoon mustard oil
1 tablespoon vegetable oil
1 onion, sliced
½ red bell pepper, seeded and thinly
  sliced
½ green bell pepper, seeded and thinly
  sliced
1 chayote, peeled, pitted and cut into
  strips
salt and freshly ground black pepper

1 Shell the shrimp and place the shells in a saucepan with the water and ginger. Simmer, uncovered, for 15 minutes until reduced by half. Strain into a pitcher and discard the shells.

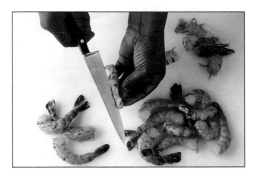

2 Devein the shrimp, place in a bowl and season with the curry powder, garlic and salt and pepper and set aside.

3 Heat the mustard and vegetable oils in a large frying pan, add all the vegetables and stir fry for 5 minutes. Season with salt and pepper, spoon into a serving dish and keep warm.

4 Wipe out the frying pan, then add and melt the butter or margarine and sauté the shrimp for about 5 minutes or until pink. Spoon over the bed of vegetables, cover and keep warm.

5 Add the ground almonds and chili to the pan, stir fry for a few seconds and then add the reserved stock and bring to a boil. Reduce the heat, stir in the cream and simmer for a few minutes, without boiling.

6 Pour the sauce over the vegetables and shrimp before serving.

Fried Porgy in Coconut Sauce

INGREDIENTS

Serves 4

4 medium porgy or butterfish
juice of 1 lemon
1 teaspoon garlic powder
salt and freshly ground black pepper
vegetable oil, for shallow frying

For the coconut sauce

1⅞ cups water
2 thin slices fresh ginger
1 cup coconut cream
2 tablespoons vegetable oil
1 red onion, sliced
2 garlic cloves, crushed
1 green chili, seeded and thinly sliced
1 tablespoon chopped fresh cilantro
salt and freshly ground black pepper

1 Cut the fish in half and sprinkle inside and out with the lemon juice. Season with the garlic powder and salt and pepper and set aside to marinate for a few hours.

2 Heat a little oil in a large frying pan. Pat off the excess lemon juice from the fish, fry in the oil for 10 minutes, turning once. Set aside.

3 To make the sauce, place the water in a saucepan with the slices of ginger, bring to a boil and simmer until the liquid is reduced to just over 1¼ cups. Take out the ginger and reserve, then add the coconut cream to the pan and stir until the coconut has been absorbed.

4 Heat the oil in a wok or large pan and fry the onion and garlic for 2–3 minutes. Add the reserved ginger and coconut stock, the chili and cilantro, stir well and then gently lower in the fish. Simmer for 10 minutes, until the fish is cooked through. Transfer the fish to a warmed serving plate, adjust the seasoning for the sauce and pour over the fish. Serve immediately.

Donu's Lobster Piri Piri

Lobster in its shell, in true Nigerian style, flavored with dried shrimp.

INGREDIENTS

Serves2–4
2 cooked lobsters, halved
fresh cilantro sprigs, to garnish

For the piri piri sauce
4 tablespoons vegetable oil
2 onions, chopped
1 teaspoon chopped fresh ginger
1 pound fresh or canned tomatoes,
  chopped
1 tablespoon tomato paste
8 ounces cooked, peeled shrimp
2 teaspoons ground coriander
1 green chili, seeded and chopped
1 tablespoon ground dried shrimp or
  crayfish
2½ cups water
1 green bell pepper, seeded and sliced
salt and freshly ground black pepper

1 Heat the oil in a large flameproof casserole and fry the onions, ginger, tomatoes and tomato paste for 5 minutes or until the onions are soft.

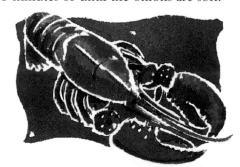

2 Add the shrimp, ground coriander, chili and ground shrimp or crayfish and stir well to mix.

3 Stir in the water, green pepper and salt and pepper, bring to a boil and simmer, uncovered, over a moderate heat for about 20–30 minutes or until the sauce is reduced.

4 Add the lobsters to the sauce and cook for a few minutes to heat through. Arrange the lobster halves on warmed serving plates and pour the sauce over each one. Garnish with cilantro sprigs and serve with fluffy white rice.

Tilapia in Turmeric, Mango and Tomato Sauce

Tilapia is widely used in African cooking, but can be found in most fishmarkets. Yam or boiled yellow plantains are good accompaniments.

INGREDIENTS

Serves 4

4 tilapia
½ lemon
2 garlic cloves, crushed
½ teaspoon dried thyme
2 tablespoons chopped scallions
vegetable oil, for shallow frying
flour, for dusting
2 tablespoons peanut oil
1 tablespoon butter or margarine
1 onion, finely chopped
3 tomatoes, peeled and finely chopped
1 teaspoon ground turmeric
4 tablespoons white wine
1 green chili, seeded and finely chopped
2½ cups strong fish stock
1 teaspoon sugar
1 medium underripe mango, peeled and diced
1 tablespoon chopped fresh parsley
salt and freshly ground black pepper

2 Heat a little vegetable oil in a large frying pan, coat the fish with some flour, then fry the fish on both sides for a few minutes until golden brown. Remove with a slotted spoon to a plate and set aside.

4 Add the turmeric, white wine, chili, fish stock and sugar, stir well and bring to a boil, then simmer gently, covered, for 10 minutes.

5 Add the fish and cook over a gentle heat for about 15–20 minutes, until the fish is cooked through. Add the mango, arranging it around the fish, and cook briefly for 1–2 minutes to heat through.

1 Place the fish in a shallow bowl, squeeze the lemon juice all over the fish and gently rub in the garlic, thyme and some salt and pepper. Place some of the scallion in the cavity of each fish, cover loosely with plastic wrap and let marinate for a few hours or overnight in the fridge.

3 Heat the peanut oil and butter or margarine in a saucepan and fry the onion for 4–5 minutes, until soft. Stir in the tomatoes and cook briskly for a few minutes.

6 Arrange the fish on a warmed serving plate with the mango and tomato sauce poured over. Garnish with chopped parsley and serve immediately.

VEGETABLE AND VEGETARIAN DISHES

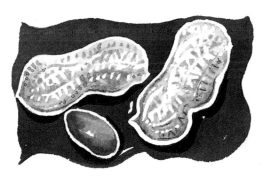

African cooks prepare lots of recipes using vegetables and pulses, and for many people these are the mainstay of their diet. Herbs and spices add an extra dimension to these dishes, frequently served with unusual and often fiery sauces. Whether you are cooking a vegetarian meal, or just want an interesting vegetable side dish, do look out for the more unusual root and green vegetables that are now available. Plantains, yams and sweet potatoes are some of the typical African vegetables that make superb dishes. Other more common vegetables, like pumpkin and corn, can, given the African treatment, be transformed into tempting and mouth-watering dishes.

Sese Plantain and Yam

INGREDIENTS

Serves 4

2 green plantains
1 pound white yam
2 tomatoes, peeled and chopped
1 red chili, seeded and chopped
1 onion, chopped
½ vegetable stock cube
1 tablespoon palm oil
1 tablespoon tomato paste
salt

1 Peel the plantains and cut into six rounds, then peel and dice the yam.

2 Place the plantains and yam in a large saucepan with 2½ cups water, bring to a boil and cook for 5 minutes. Add the tomatoes, chili and onion and simmer for another 10 minutes, then crumble in the half vegetable stock cube, stir well, cover and simmer for 5 minutes.

3 Stir in the oil and tomato paste and continue cooking for about 5 minutes or until the plantains are tender. Season with salt and pour into a warmed serving dish. Serve immediately.

COOK'S TIP

To peel the plantains, cut in half, slit the plantains along the natural ridges, then lift off the skin in sections.

Makande

A traditional dish from Tanzania, which can be served with meat, fish or simply a salad.

INGREDIENTS

Serves 3–4

1¼ cups red kidney beans, soaked overnight
1 onion, chopped
2 garlic cloves, crushed
1½ cups coconut cream
1⅓ cups frozen corn kernels
1¼ cups vegetable stock or water
salt and freshly ground black pepper

1 Drain the kidney beans and place in a saucepan, cover with water and boil rapidly for 15 minutes. Reduce the heat and continue boiling for about 1 hour, until the beans are tender, adding more water if necessary. Drain, discarding the cooking liquid.

2 Place the beans in a clean pan with the onion, garlic, coconut cream, corn and salt and pepper.

3 Add the stock or water, bring to a boil and simmer for 20 minutes, stirring occasionally to absorb the coconut cream.

4 Adjust the seasoning and spoon into a warmed serving dish. Serve with an onion and tomato salad.

Egusi Spinach and Egg

This is a superbly balanced dish for those who don't eat meat. Egusi, or ground melon seed, is widely used in West African cooking, adding a creamy texture and a nutty flavor to many recipes. It is especially good with fresh spinach.

INGREDIENTS

Serves 4

2 pounds fresh spinach
4 ounces ground egusi
6 tablespoons peanut or vegetable oil
4 tomatoes, peeled and chopped
1 onion, chopped
2 garlic cloves, crushed
1 slice fresh ginger, finely chopped
²/₃ cup vegetable stock
1 red chili, seeded and finely chopped
6 eggs
salt

1 Roll the spinach into bundles and cut into strips. Place in a bowl.

2 Cover with boiling water, then drain through a strainer. Press with your fingers to remove excess water.

3 Place the egusi in a bowl and gradually add enough water to form a paste, stirring all the time.

4 Heat the oil in a saucepan, add the tomatoes, onion, garlic and ginger and fry over a moderate heat for about 10 minutes, stirring frequently.

5 Add the egusi paste, stock, chili and salt, cook for 10 minutes, then add the spinach and stir into the sauce. Cook for 15 minutes, uncovered, stirring frequently.

6 Meanwhile hard-boil the eggs, let stand in cold water for a few minutes to cool and then shell and cut in half. Arrange in a shallow serving dish and pour the egusi spinach over the top. Serve hot.

COOK'S TIP

Instead of using boiled eggs, you could make an omelet flavored with herbs and garlic. Serve it either whole, or sliced, with the egusi sauce. If you can't find egusi, use ground almonds as a substitute.

Bean and Gari Loaf

This recipe is a newly created vegetarian dish using typically Ghanaian flavors and ingredients.

INGREDIENTS

Serves 4

1¼ cups red kidney beans, soaked overnight
1 tablespoon butter or margarine
1 onion, finely chopped
2 garlic cloves, crushed
½ red bell pepper, seeded and chopped
½ green bell pepper, seeded and chopped
1 green chili, seeded and finely chopped
1 teaspoon mixed chopped herbs
2 eggs
1 tablespoon lemon juice
5 tablespoons gari
salt and freshly ground black pepper

1 Drain the kidney beans, then place in a saucepan, cover with water and boil rapidly for 15 minutes. Reduce the heat and continue boiling for about 1 hour, until the beans are tender, adding more water if necessary. Drain, reserving the cooking liquid. Preheat the oven to 375°F and grease an 8½- x 4½-inch loaf pan.

2 Melt the butter or margarine in a large frying pan and fry the onion, garlic and peppers for 5 minutes, then add the chili, mixed herbs and a little salt and pepper.

3 Place the cooked kidney beans in a large bowl or in a food processor and mash or process to a pulp. Add the onion and pepper mixture and stir well to mix. Cool slightly, then stir in the eggs and lemon juice.

4 Place the gari in a separate bowl and sprinkle generously with warm water. The gari should become soft and fluffy after about 5 minutes.

5 Pour the gari into the bean and onion mixture and stir together thoroughly. It the consistency is too stiff, add a little of the bean liquid. Spoon the mixture into the prepared loaf pan and bake in the oven for 35–45 minutes, until firm to the touch.

6 Cool the loaf in the pan and then turn out on to a plate. Cut into thick slices and serve.

COOK'S TIP

Gari is a course-grained flour, used as a staple food, in a similar way to ground rice. Gari is made from a starchy root vegetable, cassava, which is first dried, then ground.

Black-eyed Pea Stew with Spicy Pumpkin

INGREDIENTS

Serves 3–4

1¼ cups black-eyed peas, soaked for 4
  hours or overnight
1 onion, chopped
1 green or red bell pepper, seeded and
  chopped
2 garlic cloves, chopped
1 vegetable stock cube
1 thyme sprig or 1 teaspoon dried thyme
1 teaspoon paprika
½ teaspoon allspice
2 carrots, sliced
1–2 tablespoons palm oil
salt and hot pepper sauce

For the spicy pumpkin

1½ pounds pumpkin
1 onion
2 tablespoons butter or margarine
2 garlic cloves, crushed
3 tomatoes, peeled and chopped
½ teaspoon ground cinnamon
2 teaspoons curry powder
pinch of grated nutmeg
⅔ cup water
salt, hot pepper sauce and freshly
  ground black pepper

1 Drain the peas, place in a pan and
cover generously with water. Bring
the peas to a boil.

2 Add the onion, green or red
pepper, garlic, stock cube, herbs
and spices. Simmer for 45 minutes or
until the peas are just tender. Season to
taste with the salt and a little hot
pepper sauce.

3 Add the carrots and palm oil and
continue cooking for about
10–12 minutes until the carrots are
cooked, adding a little more water if
necessary. Remove from the heat and
set aside.

4 To make the spicy pumpkin, cut
the pumpkin into cubes and finely
chop the onion.

5 Melt the butter or margarine in a
frying pan or saucepan, and add
the pumpkin, onion, garlic, tomatoes,
spices and water. Stir well to combine
and simmer until the pumpkin is soft.
Season with salt, hot pepper sauce and
black pepper, to taste. Serve with the
black-eyed peas.

Chick-peas, Sweet Potato and Garden Egg

Spicy and delicious – especially when served with Bulgur and Pine Nut Pilaf.

INGREDIENTS

Serves 3–4

3 tablespoons olive oil
1 red onion, chopped
3 garlic cloves, crushed
4 ounces sweet potatoes, peeled and diced
3 garden eggs or 1 large eggplant, diced
15-ounce can chick-peas, drained
1 teaspoon dried tarragon
½ teaspoon dried thyme
1 teaspoon ground cumin
1 teaspoon ground turmeric
½ teaspoon ground allspice
5 canned plum tomatoes, chopped with 4 tablespoons reserved juice
6 dried apricots
2½ cups strong vegetable stock
1 green chili, seeded and finely chopped
2 tablespoons chopped fresh cilantro
salt and freshly ground black pepper

1 Heat the olive oil in a large saucepan over a moderate heat. Add the onion, garlic and sweet potatoes and cook for about 5 minutes until the onion is slightly softened.

2 Stir in the garden eggs or eggplant, then add the chick-peas and the herbs and spices. Stir well to mix and cook over a gentle heat for a few minutes.

3 Add the tomatoes and their juice, the apricots, stock, chili and seasoning. Stir well, bring slowly to a boil and cook for about 15 minutes.

4 When the sweet potatoes are tender, add the cilantro, stir and adjust the seasoning if necessary.

--- COOK'S TIP ---

Garden egg is a small variety of eggplant used widely in West Africa. It is round and white, which may explain its name. You can peel the eggplant for this dish if preferred, although it's not necessary. Either white or orange sweet potatoes can be used and you can add fewer chick-peas, if you wish.

SIDE DISHES

Although some classic vegetable dishes, like sweet potatoes and plantains are served by themselves, many African side dishes are a combination of vegetables, herbs and spices. A staple food like fu fu or ground rice is always served with a meal but other side dishes can be served as well. Fu fu is a traditional African dish and can be made using various flours or root vegetables depending on the local custom. I've used yam and plantains in my recipe, which give it a pleasant mellow flavor that goes well with the meat and poultry dishes. Breads, such as Mandazi or Coconut Chappatis are popular in many parts of the African continent, eaten either with the meal or as snacks during the day.

Bulgur and Pine Nut Pilaf

Pilaf is a popular staple in the Middle East, here is a North African version.

INGREDIENTS

Serves 4
2 tablespoons olive oil
1 onion, chopped
1 garlic clove, crushed
1 teaspoon ground saffron or turmeric
1/2 teaspoon ground cinnamon
1 green chili, seeded and chopped
2 1/2 cups vegetable stock
2/3 cups white wine
1 1/3 cups bulgur
1 tablespoon butter or margarine
2–3 tablespoons pine nuts
2 tablespoons chopped fresh parsley

1 Heat the oil in a saucepan and fry the onion until soft. Add the garlic, saffron or turmeric, ground cinnamon, and chopped chili, and fry for a few seconds more.

2 Add the stock and wine, bring to a boil, then simmer for about 8 minutes.

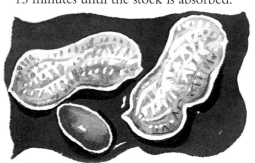

3 Rinse the bulgur under cold water, drain and add to the stock. Cover and simmer gently for about 15 minutes until the stock is absorbed.

4 Melt the butter in a small pan, add the pine nuts and fry for a few minutes until golden. Add to the bulgur with the chopped parsley and stir with a fork to mix.

5 Spoon into a warmed serving dish and serve with Chick-peas, Sweet Potato and Garden Egg or other vegetable or meat stew.

--- COOK'S TIP ---

You can leave out the wine, if you prefer, and replace with water or stock. It's not essential, but it adds extra flavor.

Joloff Rice

INGREDIENTS

Serves 4
2 tablespoons vegetable oil
1 large onion, chopped
2 garlic cloves, crushed
2 tablespoons tomato paste
1 1/2 cups long grain rice
1 green chili, seeded and chopped
2 1/2 cups vegetable or chicken stock

1 Heat the oil in a saucepan and fry the onion and garlic for 4–5 minutes until soft. Add the tomato paste and fry over a moderate heat for about 3 minutes, stirring constantly.

2 Rinse the rice in cold water, drain well and add to the pan with the chili and a pinch of salt. Cook for 2–3 minutes, stirring constantly to prevent the rice sticking to the bottom of the pan.

3 Add the stock, cover and simmer for about 15 minutes.

4 When the liquid is nearly absorbed, cover the rice with a piece of foil, cover the pan and steam over a low heat until the rice is cooked.

Efua's Ghanaian Salad

INGREDIENTS

Serves 4

4 ounces cooked, peeled shrimp
1 garlic clove, crushed
½ tablespoon vegetable oil
2 eggs
1 yellow plantain, halved
4 lettuce leaves
2 tomatoes
1 red bell pepper
1 avocado
juice of 1 lemon
1 carrot
7-ounce can tuna or sardines
1 green chili, finely chopped
2 tablespoons chopped scallion
salt and freshly ground black pepper

1 Put the shrimp in a small bowl, add the garlic and a little seasoning.

2 Heat the oil in a small saucepan, add the shrimp and cook over a low heat for a few minutes. Transfer to a plate to cool.

3 Hard-boil the eggs, place in cold water to cool, then shell and cut into slices.

4 Boil the plantain in a pan of water for 15 minutes, cool, then peel and slice thickly.

5 Shred the lettuce and arrange on a large serving plate. Slice the tomatoes and red pepper and peel and slice the avocado, sprinkling it with a little lemon juice. Arrange vegetables on the plate. Cut the carrot into matchstick-size pieces and arrange over the lettuce with the other vegetables.

6 Add the plantain, eggs, shrimp and tuna or sardines. Sprinkle with the remaining lemon juice, sprinkle the chili and scallion on top and season with salt and pepper to taste. Serve as a luncheon salad or as a side dish.

--- COOK'S TIP ---

To make a complete meal, serve this salad with a meat or fish dish. Vary the ingredients, use any canned fish and a mixture of attractive lettuce leaves.

Plantain and Green Banana Salad

The plantains and bananas may be cooked in their skins to retain their soft texture. They will then absorb all the flavor of the dressing.

INGREDIENTS

Serves 4
2 firm yellow plantains
3 green bananas
1 garlic clove, crushed
1 red onion
1–2 tablespoons chopped fresh cilantro
3 tablespoons sunflower oil
1½ tablespoons malt vinegar
salt and coarse-grain black pepper

1 Slit the plantains and bananas lengthwise along their natural ridges, then cut in half and place in a large saucepan.

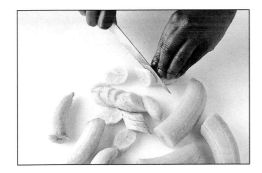

2 Cover the plantains and bananas with water, add a little salt and bring to a boil. Boil gently for 20 minutes until tender, then remove from the water. When they are cool enough to handle, peel and cut into medium-size slices.

3 Put the plantain and banana slices into a bowl and add the garlic, turning to mix.

4 Halve the onion and slice thinly. Add to the bowl with the cilantro, oil, vinegar and seasoning. Toss together to mix, then serve as an accompaniment to a main dish.

Cameroon Coconut Rice

This version of a favorite African dish, Coconut Joloff, can be left moist, like a risotto, or cooked longer for a drier result.

INGREDIENTS

Serves 4

2 tablespoons vegetable oil
1 onion, chopped
2 tablespoons tomato paste
2½ cups coconut milk
2 carrots
1 yellow bell pepper
1 teaspoon dried thyme
½ teaspoon ground allspice
1 fresh green chili, seeded and chopped
1½ cups long grain rice
salt

1 Heat the oil in a large saucepan and fry the onion for 2 minutes. Add the tomato paste and cook over a moderate heat for 5–6 minutes, stirring constantly. Add the coconut milk, stir well and bring to a boil.

2 Coarsely chop the carrots and chop the pepper, discarding the seeds.

3 Stir the carrots, pepper, thyme, allspice, chili and rice into the onion mixture, season with salt and bring to a boil. Cover and cook over a low heat until the rice has absorbed most of the liquid. Cover the rice with foil, secure with the lid and steam very gently until the rice is done. Serve hot.

Chick-pea and Okra Fry

Other vegetables can be added to this stir-fry to make a pleasing side dish. Mushrooms, cooked potatoes, zucchini or green beans would all be suitable additions.

INGREDIENTS

Serves 4

1 pound okra
1 tablespoon vegetable oil
1 tablespoon mustard oil
1 tablespoon butter or margarine
1 onion, finely chopped
1 garlic clove, crushed
2 tomatoes, finely chopped
1 green chili, seeded and finely chopped
2 slices fresh ginger
1 teaspoon ground cumin
1 tablespoon chopped fresh cilantro
15-ounce can chick-peas, drained
salt and freshly ground black pepper

1 Wash and dry the okra, remove the ends and chop coarsely.

2 Heat the vegetable and mustard oils and the butter or margarine in a large frying pan.

3 Fry the onion and garlic for 5 minutes until the onion is slightly softened. Add the chopped tomatoes, chili and ginger and stir well, then add the okra, cumin and cilantro. Simmer for 5 minutes, stirring frequently, then stir in the chick-peas and a little seasoning.

4 Cook gently for a few minutes for the chick-peas to heat through, then spoon into a serving bowl and serve at once.

Tanzanian Vegetable Rice

Serve this tasty rice with baked chicken, or a fish dish and a delicious fresh relish – Kachumbali. The vegetables are added towards the end of cooking, so that they retain their crisp texture.

INGREDIENTS

Serves 4

1½ cups basmati rice
3 tablespoons vegetable oil
1 onion, chopped
2 garlic cloves, crushed
3 cups vegetable stock or water
⅔ cup corn
½ red or green bell pepper, chopped
1 large carrot, grated
Kachumbali, to serve

1 Wash the rice in a strainer under cold water, then let drain for about 15 minutes.

2 Heat the oil in a large saucepan and fry the onion for a few minutes over a moderate heat until just soft.

3 Add the rice and stir-fry for about 10 minutes, taking care to keep stirring constantly so that the rice doesn't stick to the pan.

4 Add the garlic and the stock or water and stir well. Bring to a boil and cook over a high heat for 5 minutes, then reduce the heat, cover and cook the rice for 20 minutes.

5 Sprinkle the corn over the rice, then spread the pepper on top and then sprinkle over the grated carrot.

6 Cover tightly and steam over a low heat until the rice is cooked, then mix together with a fork and serve immediately.

COOK'S TIP

If the rice begins to dry out, add a little more stock or water, but make sure not to overcook the rice – it should be tender but not soft.

Kenyan Mung Bean Stew

The Kenyan name for this simple and tasty stew is *Dengu*.

INGREDIENTS

Serves 4

1¼ cups mung beans, soaked
   overnight
2 tablespoons ghee or butter
2 garlic cloves, crushed
1 red onion, chopped
2 tablespoons tomato paste
½ green bell pepper, seeded and cut
   into small cubes
½ red bell pepper, seeded and cut into
   small cubes
1 green chili, seeded and finely chopped

1 Put the mung beans in a large saucepan, cover with water and boil until the beans are very soft and the water has evaporated. Remove from the heat and mash with a fork or potato masher until smooth.

2 Heat the ghee or butter in a separate saucepan, add the garlic and onion and fry for 4–5 minutes until golden brown, then add the tomato paste and cook for another 2–3 minutes, stirring constantly.

3 Stir in the mashed beans, then the green and red peppers and chili.

4 Add 1¼ cups water, stirring well to mix all the ingredients together.

5 Pour back into a clean saucepan and simmer for about 10 minutes, then spoon into a serving dish and serve at once.

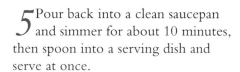

— COOK'S TIP —

Mung beans can be found in most Asian stores. If unavailable, use whole green lentils instead.

Yam Fries

INGREDIENTS

Serves 4

1 pound white yam
good pinch of chili powder or cayenne
   pepper
salt and freshly ground black pepper
oil, for deep frying

1 Peel the yam and cut into slices, then into chips. Place the yam chips in a saucepan and cover with cold salted water.

2 Bring the water to a boil, cook for 5 minutes, then drain the chips in a colander or on paper towels for 5 minutes. Sprinkle with chili powder or cayenne pepper.

— COOK'S TIP —

Only half-fill the pan with oil, as it will bubble up when the fries are added.

3 Heat the oil in a heavy saucepan or deep-fat fryer until hot, then fry the yam chips for about 6–8 minutes, until cooked through, golden brown and crisp.

4 Drain well, then turn into a dish lined with paper towels. Sprinkle with salt and serve at once.

Yam and Plantain Fu Fu

INGREDIENTS

Serves 4

1 pound white yam
2 green plantains
1 tablespoon butter or margarine
salt and black or white pepper

1 Peel, wash and slice the yam and place in a saucepan, then cover with cold salted water.

2 Cut the green plantains in half, slit along the natural ridges in three places and remove the skins. Put the plantains in the saucepan with the yam, bring to a boil and cook for 25 minutes or until tender.

3 Drain the vegetables and place in a blender or food processor. Add the butter or margarine, season well with salt and pepper, and process until smooth and lump free.

4 Turn the fu fu into a bowl, then take small handfuls and shape into balls. Serve with casseroles and stews.

— COOK'S TIP —

Yam Fu Fu is especially good served with Groundnut Soup, and Fish and Okra Soup. You could serve the soup and Yam Fu Fu instead of a main meal.

Ethiopian Collard Greens

Also known as *Abesha Gomen*, this dish is simple and delicious. Spinach can be used in place of the collard greens if desired.

INGREDIENTS

Serves 4
1 pound collard greens
4 tablespoons olive oil
2 small red onions, finely chopped
1 garlic clove, crushed
½ teaspoon grated fresh ginger
2 green chilies, seeded and sliced
⅔ cup vegetable stock or water
1 red bell pepper, seeded and sliced
salt and freshly ground black pepper

1 Wash the collard greens, then strip the leaves from the stalks and steam the leaves over a pan of boiling water for about 5 minutes or until slightly wilted. Set aside on a plate to cool, then place in a strainer or colander and press out the excess water.

2 Using a large sharp knife, slice the collard greens very thinly.

3 Heat the oil in a saucepan and fry the onions until browned. Add the garlic and ginger and stir-fry with the onions for a few minutes, then add the chilies and a little of the stock or water and cook for 2 minutes.

4 Add the greens, red pepper and the remaining stock or water. Season with salt and pepper, mix well, then cover and cook over a low heat for about 15 minutes.

COOK'S TIP

Traditionally this dish is cooked with more liquid and for longer. The cooking time has been reduced from 45 minutes to 15 minutes. However, if you fancy a more authentic taste, cook for longer and increase the amount of liquid. Green cabbage is a good substitute for collard greens.

Green Lentil Salad

Azifa is the African name for this piquant, colorful salad.

INGREDIENTS

Serves 4
1 cup green lentils, soaked overnight
2 tomatoes, peeled and chopped
1 red onion, finely chopped
1 green chili, seeded and chopped
4 tablespoons lemon juice
5 tablespoons olive oil
½ teaspoon prepared mustard
salt and freshly ground black pepepr

1 Place the lentils in a saucepan, cover with water and bring to a boil. Simmer for 45 minutes until soft, drain, then turn into a bowl and mash lightly with a potato masher.

2 Add the tomatoes, onion, chili, lemon juice, olive oil, mustard and seasoning. Mix well, adjust seasoning if necessary, then chill before serving as an accompaniment to a meat or fish dish.

Kachumbali Salad

Kachumbali is a peppery relish from Tanzania, where it is served with grilled meat or fish dishes, together with rice – this salad uses the same combination of flavors.

INGREDIENTS

Serves 4–6
2 red onions
4 tomatoes
1 green chili
¹/₂ cucumber
1 carrot
juice of 1 lemon
salt and freshly ground black pepper

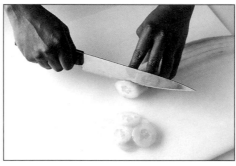

1 Slice the onions and tomatoes very thinly and place in a bowl.

2 Slice the chili lengthwise, discard the seeds, then chop very finely. Peel and slice the cucumber and carrot and add to the onions and tomatoes.

3 Squeeze the lemon juice over the salad. Season with salt and freshly ground black pepper and toss together to mix. Serve as an accompaniment, salad or relish.

———— COOK'S TIP ————

Traditional *Kachumbali* is made by very finely chopping the onions, tomatoes, cucumber and carrot which produces a very moist, sauce-like mixture. This is good served inside chappatis, and eaten as a salad roll.

Coconut Relish

This simple but delicious relish is widely made in Tanzania. Only the white part of the coconut flesh is used.

INGREDIENTS

Makes about 2 ounces
2 ounces fresh or dried coconut
2 teaspoons lemon juice
¹/₄ teaspoon salt
2 teaspoons water
¹/₄ teaspoon finely chopped red chili

1 Grate the coconut and place in a mixing bowl. If using dried coconut, add just enough water to moisten.

2 Add the lemon juice, salt, water and chili. Stir thoroughly and serve as a relish with meats or as an accompaniment to a main dish.

DESSERTS

In a continent like Africa, where fruit is cheap, plentiful and completely fresh, it's not surprising that it's eaten at any time of the day, whenever people fancy. Market stalls are full of luscious fruit – pineapples, mangoes and spicy smelling guavas – and it's not unusual for fruit trees to grow in your garden, there just for the picking. Fruit is also served at the end of the meal but desserts are not a strong feature of African cuisine and apart from Banana Mandazi, most of the recipes in this section are my own creations. My resistance level to coconut is low, hence its presence in many of the recipes. If you're not as partial to it as me, use it a little more moderately!

Fresh Pineapple with Coconut

This refreshing dessert can also be made with canned pineapple. This makes a good substitute, but fresh is best.

Ingredients

Serves 4

1 fresh pineapple, peeled
slivers of fresh coconut
1¼ cups pineapple juice
4 tablespoons coconut liqueur
1-inch piece preserved ginger, plus
  3 tablespoons of the syrup

1 Peel and slice the pineapple, arrange in a serving dish and sprinkle the coconut slivers on top.

2 Place the pineapple juice and coconut liqueur in a saucepan and heat gently.

3 Thinly slice the ginger and add to the pan along with the ginger syrup. Bring just to a boil and then simmer gently until the liquid is slightly reduced and the sauce is fairly thick.

4 Pour the sauce over the pineapple and coconut, let cool, then chill before serving.

Cook's Tip

If fresh coconut is not available, then use dried coconut instead.

Spiced Nutty Bananas

Cinnamon and nutmeg are spices which perfectly complement bananas in this delectable dessert.

INGREDIENTS

Serves 3

6 ripe, but firm, bananas
2 tablespoons chopped unsalted cashew nuts
2 tablespoons chopped unsalted peanuts
2 tablespoons dried coconut
½–1 tablespoon raw sugar
1 teaspoon ground cinnamon
½ teaspoon freshly grated nutmeg
²/₃ cup orange juice
4 tablespoons rum
1 tablespoon butter or margarine
heavy cream, to serve

1 Preheat the oven to 400°F. Slice the bananas and place in a greased, shallow ovenproof dish.

2 Mix together the cashew nuts, peanuts, coconut, sugar, cinnamon and nutmeg in a small bowl.

3 Pour the orange juice and rum over the bananas, then sprinkle with the nut and sugar mixture.

4 Dot the top with butter or margarine, then bake in the oven for 15–20 minutes or until the bananas are golden and the sauce is bubbly. Serve with heavy cream.

— COOK'S TIP —

Freshly grated nutmeg makes all the difference to this dish. More rum can be added if preferred. Chopped mixed nuts can be used instead of peanuts.

Banana and Melon in Orange Vanilla Sauce

Most large supermarkets and health food stores sell vanilla beans. If vanilla beans are hard to find, use a few drops of natural vanilla extract instead.

INGREDIENTS

Serves 4

1¼ cups orange juice
1 vanilla bean or a few drops vanilla extract
1 teaspoon grated orange rind
1 tablespoon sugar
4 bananas
1 honeydew melon
2 tablespoons lemon juice

1 Place the orange juice in a small saucepan with the vanilla bean, orange rind and sugar and gently bring to a boil.

2 Reduce the heat and simmer gently for 15 minutes or until the sauce is syrupy. Remove from the heat and set aside to cool. If using vanilla extract, stir into the sauce once it has cooled.

3 Coarsely chop the bananas and melon, place in a large serving bowl and toss with the lemon juice.

4 Pour the cooled sauce over the fruit and chill before serving.

Banana Mandazi

INGREDIENTS

Serves 4

1 egg
2 ripe bananas, coarsely chopped
⅔ cup milk
½ teaspoon vanilla extract
2 cups self-rising flour
1 teaspoon baking powder
3 tablespoons sugar
vegetable oil, for deep frying

1 Place the egg, bananas, milk, vanilla extract, flour, baking powder and sugar in a blender or food processor.

2 Process to make a smooth batter. It should have a creamy pourable consistency. If it is too thick, add a little extra milk. Set aside for 10 minutes.

3 Heat the oil in a heavy saucepan or deep-fat fryer. When hot, carefully place spoonfuls of the mixture in the oil and fry for 3–4 minutes until golden. Remove with a slotted spoon and drain on paper towels. Keep warm while cooking the remaining mandazis, then serve at once.

Tropical Fruit Pancakes

INGREDIENTS

Serves 4

1 cup self–rising flour
pinch of grated nutmeg
1 tablespoon superfine sugar
1 egg
1¼ cups milk
1 tablespoon melted butter or
   margarine, plus extra for frying
1 tablespoon fine dried coconut
   (optional)
fresh cream, to serve

For the filling

8 ounces ripe, firm mango
2 bananas
2 kiwi fruit
1 large orange
1 tablespoon lemon juice
2 tablespoons orange juice
1 tablespoon honey
2–3 tablespoons orange liqueur
   (optional)

1 Sift the flour, nutmeg and superfine sugar into a large bowl. In a separate bowl, beat the egg lightly, then beat in most of the milk. Add to the flour mixture and beat with a wooden spoon to mix to a thick, smooth batter.

2 Add the remaining milk, butter and coconut, if using, and continue beating until the batter is smooth and of a fairly thin, pourable consistency.

3 Melt a little butter or margarine in a large nonstick frying pan. Swirl to cover the pan, then pour in a little batter to cover the bottom of the pan. Fry until golden brown, then toss or turn with a spatula. Repeat with the remaining mixture to make about eight pancakes.

4 Dice the mango, coarsely chop the bananas and slice the kiwi fruit. Cut away the peel and pith from the orange and cut into segments.

5 Place the fruit in a bowl. Mix the lemon and orange juices, honey and orange liqueur, if using, then pour over the fruit.

6 Spoon a little fruit down the center of a pancake and fold over each side. Repeat with the remaining pancakes, then serve with fresh cream.

Papaya and Mango with Mango Cream

INGREDIENTS

Serves 4
2 large ripe mangoes
1¼ cups extra thick heavy cream
8 dried apricots, halved
⅔ cup orange juice or water
1 ripe papaya

1 Take one thick slice from one of the mangoes and, while still on the skin, slash the flesh with a sharp knife in a criss-cross pattern to make cubes.

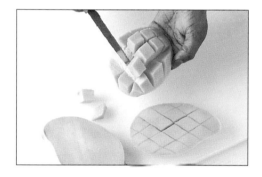

2 Turn the piece of mango inside-out and cut away the cubed flesh from the skin. Place in a bowl, mash with a fork to a pulp, then add the cream and mix together well. Spoon into a freezer container and freeze for about 1–1½ hours until half frozen.

3 Meanwhile, put the apricots and orange juice or water in a small saucepan. Bring to a boil, then simmer gently until the apricots are soft, adding a little more juice or water if necessary, so that the apricots remain moist. Remove the pan from the heat and set aside to cool.

4 Chop or dice the remaining mangoes as above and place in a bowl. Cut the papaya in half, remove the seeds and peel. Dice the flesh and add to the mango.

5 Pour the apricot sauce over the fruit and gently toss together so the fruit is well coated.

6 Stir the half-frozen mango cream a few times until spoonable but not soft. Serve the fruit topped with the mango cream.

COOK'S TIP

Mangoes vary tremendously in size. If you can only find small ones, buy three instead of two to use in this dessert.

Index